REMNANTS OF HANNAH

Books by Dara Wier

Remnants of Hannah
Reverse Rapture
Hat on a Pond
Voyages in English
Our Master Plan
Blue for the Plough
The Book of Knowledge
All You Have in Common
The 8-Step Grapevine
Blood, Hook & Eye

Limited Editions

Fly on the Wall
(X in Fix)

REMNANTS OF HANNAH

DARA WIER

WAVE BOOKS

SEATTLE / NEW YORK

Published by Wave Books
www.wavepoetry.com

Wave Books titles are distributed to the trade by
Consortium Book Sales and Distribution
1045 Westgate Drive, St. Paul, Minnesota 55114

Library of Congress Cataloging-in-Publication Data:

Wier, Dara
  Remnants of Hannah / Dara Wier.—1st ed.
      p. cm.
  Poems.   —
  ISBN 1-933517-08-5 (trade pbk. : alk. paper)—ISBN 1-933517-09-3
(alk. paper)
  I. Title.

PS3573.I357R46 2006
811'.54—dc22

2006000037

Designed and composed by J. Johnson.
Printed in the United States of America

9 8 7 6 5 4 3 2 1

First Edition

Wave Books 005

for Emily
for Guy
for Jim

Contents

I shall not go 'til I hear from you.

— E. A. Poe

Attitude of Rags

It felt like a story sorry it'd lost all its sentences,
Like a sentence looking for its syntax.
All of the words had homeless, unemployed, orphan
Written all over their faces.
It had that parboiled, simmering, half-baked look
Of curiosity about its mouth, like a month of Sundays
Has in the mind of a non-believer, a true back-slider.
One got the impression reluctance was waxing.
One wanted to say passion was taking a beating.
One wanted to say one's prey to one's feelings.
The feathers of their feelings were all scattered.
It was the kind of day were one to see a flock of
Creepy baby angel heads attached at their necks to
Pitch-black aerodynamically preposterous little wings
Clustering at the sum of things, one would rub one's
Eyes, be too faint to respond, much less explain.
It looked the way a fence looks just after the last
Stampede. A big old blood-colored barn collapsed in
Its tracks. Out of hiding came all the hidden cameras.
It looked like streets look after a parade's disbanded.
It was the kind of day in which emotions roaming from
Town to town, free to be themselves, enjoyed their
Rich fantasy lives. This was the kind of day that day
Was. We were rags in the hands of a narcoleptic duster.

That Vagrant Mistral Vexing the Sun: a far cry

I washed my brain and hung it to dry
In a steady breeze on a black clothes line.
I put a blanket down where it looked as if
The sun would be for a few hours more.
I stood by a long way off, on a tower,
On a rock, on a rooftop made of glass.
I remembered half of bible history in reverse,
I watched myself go back to being a romance
Between two hellbent cells.
I followed an earthworm as far into its vermiform
Home as it would let me go.
I followed ants carrying nearly invisible separate
Parts of something they wanted to carry back.
I no longer had a face, if I ever did.
The angle of the sun showed me shadows of things
I'd never seen.
I looked at my hands through a magnifying lens
Long enough for smoke to emerge.
I wouldn't need that brain again, I left it
For birds, in lieu of words, and seeds.

Independence Day

We'd incorporated a laundry lending motion
Detector into the third figure without success.
Everyone commenced dispersing themselves back
To their homes all dejected.
Many fires were set, much ice was cut, a few
Links fell away, a key attached to a braided
Horsehair bracelet got left behind, many more
Samples went into a sample case, midnight unbraided.
Everyone spent the next three days practicing
Free will. They insisted on it. They lived by it.
Was there any other way? That's one thing we wanted
To know. And if there were where would we find it?
Oh, maybe just over there, over the edge of that
Precipice. If no one volunteers we can draw straws.
Everyone spent the next several hours in deep reasoning.
Or at least made it look as if that were what we were
Doing. Then we drew straws to elect a new leader.
Something we suspected not all that pretty was happening
In the cellar. That would have to be saved for later.
We called for a consensus and sure enough we found it.
It looked as if it were perfect. But was it a solution?
Everyone spent the next several days in denial.
Or at least that's what our leader said we were in—

Then we drew straws to elect a new leader.
And sure enough once again it was our old leader who
Drew the shortest straw. And we were back to square one.
But we refused to call it that, we called it progress.
You idiots, our leader said, what have you done with the
Consensus? This caused us every one to become exceedingly
Sheepish. We who'd been so thoroughly entrusted had
Allowed ourselves to be mightily distracted.
Everyone spent the next several months hanging crepe.
That's what our leader said we should do for the rest
Of our lives. So we drew straws to elect a new leader.
No, we set the straw on fire, it started in the cellar,
Old milk cartons, filters, dead animals, it was a
Ghoul's soup down there, and we made up glorious anthems
To praise the courage of our leader.

A Search for an Opposite Inescapable Conclusion

I took a deep breath, sighed, took my symbol
Out of storage and sat there thinking:
I put my symbol on and started sewing:
But we had not been to the drygoods store,
We had no thread: still it felt and looked
Like sewing: but we had no cloth: still
We were following a pattern: but it didn't
Seem to be visible: still we could see some
Thing gaining shape: but it wasn't what
We'd imagined: still throughout the afternoon
And into the evening we kept at it: sewing
Neverendingly as a steady line of ants, trans-
Lucent zorapterans, filed across the forest floor:
But we did not know where they were going and
Had been told they were of no economic interest:
Still a gradual lightening of radial basting we
Continued to be sewing: or so it seemed for we
Tacked and we laced and we hemmed in reverse:
We peered through our eyeglasses of bullet-proof
Glass: still we saw a pair of scissors put through
Its paces: but we had not been to the drygoods
Store so were we unable to transport rotations:
Our symbol had been in our family for 49 generations:
It was on the end of the invisible stick God used

To write his name in the dirt: it was on the end
Of the invisible stick God used to write our initials
Next to last on his shopping list: the rococo taste,
Insane coloring, forever dreaming undisturbed by
Reality:

Last Words

Sometimes birds brush aside words
Every once in a while one finds a sword in a shrub
Once in a whale there is a table floating & flailing
With a candle burning in a candle holder with a handle
On it
As things turned out it was you I cared for the most
So I look to you for advice where you are
And you give me back silence and a blue glass of water
And dust
It's a wonder while smoke ascends in that timeless way
It does, anyone ever gets anything done
It took someone most of all of a year to finish a simple
Sentence, aye, to sift through all the cool ashes
Aye, to steady evenhandedly a bucket of water with
A tiny blue boat on its surface
You give me the time and the place and the suitcase
You give me what have you
You grant me a sequence of wishes, a map you've dotted
With sequins, and the other half of a sentence
It never took a lot of practice to do penance
An obsolete musical instrument has a sad sound to it
Like a bolt out of the blue sometimes you whistled
Not for long, not too loud, never a tune I knew
Once you whistled to keep a tunnel we were crossing

From collapsing
You give me the coordinates and the conditions
You let me see the standards
You put your blanket down where you wanted me to be
You were the captain of all of your stories
I was a horse always racing to be within an inch
Out of reach of some trouble
I always found the best things when you had forgotten
All about me until you remembered and came back to find
Me right where you'd left me
I wonder how many hours we stood on the decks of the
Ferries
I remember you most in the morning
Aye, and the tiny blue boat has a horse standing on
Its deck
And there's a bird with an envelope in its beak
Standing on the horse's back
And there's an ant, no, it's a spider dropping
By a thread from where the envelope is sealed
It's dropping to the deck, it's spidering under
The rail
I whistle for the horse to come over, I can smell
How much hay it's eaten
The crazy bird won't let go of the envelope
The last words are crazy bird

Early Morning Ecological Radio

And the ones they wanted most
would have fluorescent orange eyes.
The new bridge would be beautiful,
its cables would be woven by spiders.
Leeches and maggots were back in business
doing for us what they'd always done,
or doing for themselves some things we found
beneficial.
In that life I was held together with hedgehog spine.
Some seeds choose not to germinate for hundreds of
years. That's up to them.
Aren't there some things you wouldn't tell a soul?
It's strange though because you wind up talking to
yourself and there seem to be at least two of you,
sometimes agreeing, sometimes getting into a twisted
bitch. As if you were a kid, back in the wild,
making up a world you sometimes ruled, and sometimes
you had to hide.
When they say one hand isn't telling the other hand
what it's doing, what are they saying? Maybe they're
praying for rain, maybe for rain to go away & rain
somewhere else, it's hard to say.
We tried to bend without buckling & now & then we did.
A past without precedent is the only one it's safe to

visit, we can be one another there without damage, we
can slip into one another's skin.

Pass the garden, please.

We'd spotted a band of insurgent analysands rotating
introspectively into the farm belt.

Once I became accustomed to it, it was good
to have eight legs.

When next we meet I will have sewn for you
a stunningly simple shirt.

As if it were the last living shirt on earth.

Those Generals' Eyes

When I was always the same, someone says,
I was always me. Of course you are, you were,
Someone blurs back, someone shares, as someone
Says, something terrifyingly weird about them-
Selves, something along the lines of if it were up
To me I'd kill us all to spare the pain, not that
Exactly, something worse, something I won't say,
Someone says when I saw them holding hands, says
I wanted to be them then and not be me holding
A different hand, says see, see I looked at who
I was, I saw someone I'd never want to be, some
Of us didn't know what to say, we were speechless,
Our ransacked brains were wild inside their orders,
A full-blooded moon was foaming in our faces.

For a Chinese Poet Writing Through the Night Up on the Edge of Mt. Pollux

Now I could see I'd been stirring the pot
For almost ten thousand years.
I could see I'd be stirring forever.
So far nothing'd changed.
Nobody appeared.
I stirred myself into a bottomless sleep,
I was the smallest thing in the world.
Fragment of spit, rumor of mud.
Something that almost might have been.
I no longer had skin or fine hairs along
My arms for wind to chill or an ant to wander
Over. I no longer had friends.
No sister, no brother.
I hadn't cried when my father & my mother
Waved goodbye and their ship exited the harbor.
I hadn't asked them where they were going.
They left me no instructions.

Clairsentient Goat

I wish someone would remind me what happened to my legs,
I can still feel the hand that took me down from the shelf,
I crossed a bridge in the pocket of a coat,
I liked how their music drowned everything out,
For a long time I stayed behind a sugar bowl on a table
Next to a windowledge,
I didn't speak anyone's language,
It took a long time to see all the way down,
Somewhere in the distance there was part of a boat,
I don't know where they went at night,
As if a bottomless body of water were at work,
As if they might never come back,
Sometimes I could watch a woman hoeing,
Some of the trees were covered with leaves,
I felt part of an earthquake, it was very early in the
Morning, I picked up three different warnings,
I couldn't get to the children who were crying,
There was sugar all over the table,
I could hear them under their pillows where they were
Hiding, I wanted my legs back, I asked the ants if
They had seen them before they crossed the river,
I wanted my legs back, I tried to reach the dispatcher
Who stood in a box by the ferry, ants never have
More than one thing on their minds,

Note on a wave, one drop of blood, one leg at a time,
I can feel the hand that put me down on this ledge.

Injured Books

Near the top of each page a new story would begin, go on for a while, reach the end of the page, and never end. One would become lost in story after story, set on edge, anxious to find out what would finally happen. And always, nothing, no matter where one found oneself in any story at the end of the page it was over. You would never know how each story might have ended. At the end of the page it was over. We took these books with us to our desert islands.

Faux Self-Portrait of You

You are a very uneven person.
You, on the other hand, the one with not quite
five fingers, are a very uneven person.
Look me in the eye I say with conviction and say
you are a person of complete unevenness.
I look away to look for the surface of something
whose unevenness is its main attraction.
Very uneven person, I address you haphazardly,
you are a patchy, jerky lurcher.
You are nonuniform. You are subsubsubstantial,
I say to you of the fluctuating essence of uneven-
ness. No, I say, I am not a triangle, I do not
fit in the corner. I am an uneven piece of furn-
iture. There is a sirocco in you today.
You are a difficult table. Anything that rolls
rolls off of you almost immediately.
You're not good for a broken string of beads,
Is this not so I say uneven person that you are.
I look down to watch the beads roll where the floor
leans. An odd lullaby passes through my hair.

The Limestone of the Continent Consists of Infinite Masses

First a man tells me what it's like
to build a coffin for his friend, quickly.
Next a friend tells me what it's like to
lose another baby.
Then I pass a baby parked in a stroller
with nobody in sight watching over her.
No one in earshot patrolling or guarding.
Maybe I've stumbled across an abandoned baby.
Maybe whoever's left her unguarded believes
in guardian angels.
Yesterday we said goodbye to a greyhound.
I was signing in blood marks on every corner.
Maybe the baby will turn into an unreachable soldier.

Incident on the Road to the Capital

A wolf had grown tired of his character and sought
to find a means to transform himself into something
more vicious, more deadly. While his coat was slick,
thick and well-colored, for he was an excellent hunter,
he yearned for something to do that had nothing to do
with survival or instinct. He no longer killed because
he needed to or could. All that was useless, too practical,
too obvious. He wanted to kill for some other purpose.
For all of his successfully completed kills, his perfect
record of stealth and elusion, he felt nothing. When he
ran into me the other day on his journey to consult the
oracle of escalated suffering we shared a table in the
shade of a parasol tree in whose branches were preening
half a dozen or so birds with gaudy chromatic feathers.
A few of these fell onto the dome of his forehead but he
was too engrossed in his story to brush them away. He
didn't look like a very serious wolf. I think he was
missing a real opportunity.

Prose Poem

For a long time I'd wanted to be in a prose
poem and could find no way to do so that
I despaired I'd ever get to but here I am now
and I will not leave here until my desire to
be in a prose poem is satisfied and so I will
not stray out of this prose poem even while
I don't know what to do in here and though I'm
lost when it comes to what could or should be
happening in this prose poem I will take up a
digression that involves a crazy essay recently
read about what hideous prisons paragraphs are
and how until writers find new ways around them
paragraphs will hold writers hostage and never
let them think thoughts other than thoughts para-
graphs delimit with their omnipotent paragraph
authority. So there. I'm feeling just fine now
sticking around in this prose poem giving me
a very satisfying prose poem feeling and perhaps
some time later long after I've exited this
prose poem I can look back with nostalgic poign-
ancy thanking and praising the prose poem for
allowing me to spend a short time in its precincts.
I'm now leaving this prose poem.

Homage to John Clare

Babies come into the world without shadows
Almost like snakes
Ants have better chances, ants never weep
I'm trying to talk my brain into recovering from a blow
It took from a fork made of words
By a real brain
My love saw it happen but could only exclaim he tried to
Explain something from heaven but it was from hell what
The hell it didn't hurt me it was more like being hit on
The head by a feather, a small one
To think in reverse is not possible
Or is that what is happening when one reads something
Backwards something reads one when happening is what
That is
Vinyl, it was said with authority
Llamas look as if they like grazing in the rain in the
Fields, east of town
John Clare also grazed on his way home from his asylum
I was looking at a bear standing upright in a t-shirt
Licking a page of a book it was holding
Maybe words on a page were honey or
Something bears are attracted to, like fish or
Bittersweet berries
I have no further access to the pages of that book

I have no feathers, I am not made of vinyl
I was trying to sound as if I meant business
I had the shadows
Of the leaves of a tree all over me
The sun inched over, I was covered with cobwebs
My love was suspiciously silent

Pseudo-analysis

You are a nuclear power plant manager.
You are living under an alias.
You have children you don't know you have.
You are picturing yourself as the leader of a very
powerful nation.
You say *ethical* as though it were a hot knife moving
through butter.
You have more power than you know what to do with.
More power than is good for you on a good day.
What is your motto?
You initiated a graceful diversion.
For your project you xeroxed kleenex.
Because your project was to rescue diaphanous.
There was a drop of blood moving over a map
monitoring your path.
It was just average, right for your age, within
the parameters of your percentile, you suggested.
You present yourself in a freeze frame then a series
Of whip-pans then several layers of multiple dissolves.
You sold your business, burned down your house, got
rid of your car, started walking and wound up here.
You don't know who your mother or your father are.
You don't know where you were born.
A true analysis of your character is not possible
at this time.

Of Houses I've Inhabited Forever Without Knowing

There were hallways into quarters I'd never seen.
Rooms behind rooms where no one has ever gone.
Walls with secret panels hiding vast empty realms.
A door leading to a cellar where no door has been
Before, cellar wide open with a skyblue ceiling
Across which a flock of geese is flying over a
Pale glacial lake. Sometimes I can just make out
Someone I love who's died sitting on a crate by
Its shore. Once someone was flying by and invited
Me to come along. I hadn't answered fast enough
& they were gone. Logic had slowed me down.

Healthy-minded, Uplifting, Optimistic

A single wire hanger on a nail by itself
Isn't bad though a stack of them on a floor
Is too gloomy for words. We have a sword,
It keeps us calm to polish it sometimes when we
Sit by a fire regaling one another with charms
& while we wait while blisters form on the crowns
Of our brains, slightly viridescent, with lives
Of their own. Come around and see me sometime,
Sometimes they say, check out that parallax.
Whereas, a quasi-movie with a pseudo soundtrack:
I saw it seven times—is seven still a lucky #?
I prefer nine, as in lives, as in cats escaping
Black holes. I suppose it was a burning question,
What do you say, how far away is that sun—is it
Far enough away? Infinitely far. Sometime around
2000/2001 the word *surreal* came to mean "hard to
Put into words" & "like something you'll never for-
Get in your life," and that's all, and it was a
Useful marketing device. *Device* is a cruel word,
A catch-all, with sharp edges, forged in fires.
Something as small as a book of matches, *cruel* is
A word squeezed from its juices, *juice* is a word
In some kinds of music, that's all that matters,
My wrist is around five inches around, it works

Like a charm, like someone says, say smatter that
Toast with some of that butter, it does it, like
Magic. I lost my dewclaw and have never been
Able to find it, not that it matters, I can get
By without it, though when I miss it it feels as
If neutrinos have been having their way with my
Soul. *Soul* is a word stuck on a sword, hung on a
Wall, it is a fireball, a can of worms, a
Family of curves. I don't know when will ever
Be the right time to be personalized, to be as
Is spoken, socially redeemed, like a virgule,
And/or any other oblong.

It Wasn't Exactly Like Being Left Standing at the Altar

I had on my superfine handy translation glasses
So I could see what you mean.
It was worth selling my soul for
The convenience.
To memorize comes about as easily to me as a mouse
Comes to a cat. But some things I remember.
It was a memorable evening.
So I closed my eyes and spun the globe but it
Was one of those perpetual motion globes, filled
With indecision, with minds of its own.
Remember when I told you about the memory competitions?
Remember how I made my fortune?
Once I wrote a novel & it was made into a movie &
The movie won an Oscar & licensing & franchises
Were gravy.
You remember the story?
At first I wouldn't take any money.
A sinister but lovable band of pranksters with too
Much time on their hands plot to steal everything
From out of all the time capsules there are in the world.
Nothing's too insignificant or unambitious.
They succeed. They go undetected. It's a perfect
Crime. The movie's just a lot of dialogue with them
Sitting around in a condemned movie house arguing

About what to do next.
Beats me. You're the one who left me with all that
Time to kill. No dubbing, no subtitles, that's
All I remember about the contract.
What am I telling you this for, you were my agent.

Alexia by Other Means

There were eight days in that passage of time,
Many years, though hours and minutes were gone
Where walls were standing they were staying
Corners were blurred where spiders were installed
Tables much too large to ever make it around
I wouldn't trust any chairs if I were you
I wouldn't touch any switches
Some maidenhair ferns with their specks and their fronds
A telephone ringing
The coldest cup of coffee isolated in history
Watch where gravity's let glass relax for a while
We call it the sun but that's not what it is
Long ago we went to the moon and never returned
One of our toys is on Mars tapping around
Looking for something to eat
I wouldn't open that cabinet
It would be around the third day now
Maybe a dozen years have passed
It looks as if it might be safe to sit on the staircase
If you're willing to sit there forever
I wouldn't get too close to that snakeplant
Maybe you shouldn't take off your coat
What would they keep bowls on their floor for
To lure in some owls, to entertain a few bats

I wouldn't open those blinds
No one should see that passage of time
No one should have to look
Thousands of mothwhite larvae examining my mind

The Shadows

To be like a spider a kid's captured
In a bug house and forgotten on a bench
Beneath a room inside a hemlock in the far off
Corner of a garden, then it's raining
Someone simmering
Someone sleeping in an airplane flying over the Atlantic
Flyway
We looked at a map dotted with fires and reached
For a pencil to draw lines between them to see if
A figure might emerge into which some kind of meaning
Might be assigned
There was a whooping crane for whom we'd wept
With a fish in its mouth, frowning
There was an endless chainlink fence
To be like a vine finding a fence a good enough home
To be a scrap of foil someone's fashioned into a bird
Or what passes for a bird made of foil
Every time you think of me I shudder, why else
Would I stay inside the shadows
Why else would I step aside
You were the one who asked me more than once what
Is it that makes something make sense
I think you wore that thought out until it was worn
The way a blanket a child uses to find how sleep shows
What sleep does

To be fooled-with inside a perpetual motion shuffling
Of cards, to be folded like a paper fan, to be used
To cool a face, to be clipped to spokes on a wheel
Now you tell me how sound travels as you throw a
Replica of my head over a rail into a river
It was about time. I needed to know how some thing
Worked
I liked how you made my head out of an old cannonball
I liked how you made my eyes look tired
I liked the expression of mild disbelief
You put on my face
I liked the color you used and where you put the arrows
I liked flying through the air like an arrow
I liked how you stole the cannonball from a battery
In a rainstorm in the summertime
Once we hid in a gunnery on a precipice far away
From everything
Once you let me pick what color leaves would be
Sometimes you didn't care what I was thinking
Or what my hands were up to
Or you asked me what was on my mind and there was
Nothing I could say
To be soundproof, to not breathe a word
Like water trickling through a sandtrap inside a cistern
Like a seed inside an envelope inside an icebox

Like a bandage folded on a workbench
Like something someone hands you you put inside your
Pocket
It's good you didn't tell me what was on the horizon
It took a long time though eventually I began to under-
Stand why you stayed away from fortune-tellers and
Speculators of all kinds
They always gave me the whammies
They always gave me the shivers
Once someone sent me uninvited my complete astro-
Logical chart
It felt on my back as if a sharpshooter had me in
His line of sight, as if I were rightly stalked
Don't worry, I didn't read it
I sent it back
I remember the time you loaned me your scarf
I remember the morning a ghost in a cocktail dress
Walked past us on a freezing strand of beach
I remember when you did or didn't part your hair
I remember what happened to your eyes
I liked how you made them two zeroes
I liked how you made them two galaxies
I watched the way you could cross them
You were the one with the knapsack and boat
The one with dirt on your shoes and dust on your
Shoulders
I was the one with a glass of cool water

Where Will I Put Myself for These Purposes

Mercy boiled in a pot on our stove.
Nothing was gentle about it.
We'd been handed a present so present
We were bound by great pain to preserve it.
Inside my head is no candle, there's a searchlight
In there, alarming.
Love's sometimes a weapon of mass destruction.
And what are you, a thread or a fuse?
Inside my head is a flock of sparrows at daybreak.
I'm a stray cat after some breakfast.
I'm a couple of handfuls of seed.
There's little bits of blood on the tips of my feathers.
If I were me, I'd look away from this sunrise.
I'm an army of ants up early, housecleaning.

Circumference

Anyone has the urge and the dream to begin
to go and to do whatever water and dogs and skies want
Look light right through camisoles if you want to—
Anyone's feeling sleepy in fresh perfume

One has dread and thumping and a handbook
The sea has made a mistake but that can be corrected
It would take too long to mix up all its letters
One would be inside a camel waiting to be born gold

You have no thoughts really and really are a thief
Smears you eat and there goes your heart
Fish with pimples are aggravated by your sun
You were asleep eons ago when tall warriors ate your heart

I was just small then and underneath nothing
more a chink somewhere an and a piece of a heart
someone needs someone to slather them with sunblock
I deny I'm a part of any of this

A Mirage in the Margins of Realia

I went out to where a barn had been converted
In edgewise with some wind where my hair flew
I carried an old tin bucket with holes drilled in it
Into my eyes the way lights drill into still water
By slow degrees I inched in slanted & invisible
So as not to scare the escape mechanisms deeply
Were they sleeping in shallow sleeping pools
They were scarcely evanescing as before in paradox
With one another without touching the floor
Inch by inch in a kind of gradual way I seemed
To be standing in between where breathing was
Etched into a subcatatonic wishful thinking com-
Plex with all of its raw emotional insulation
Showing me everything and then the flip side
I went into back where there were mules in the barn
There were owls lined up on the rafters
There were cats with many kittens attached
There was an army blanket draped over a haybale
A canteen with its cap on & a hole shot through it
A scythe & a whetstone, a kerosene lantern on a
Ledge, an old cow's thighbone with a mangy dog
Attached, there was the sound of water dripping
Somewhere far off in a corner, I could see the
Back of someone's head half-reflected in a shaving

Mirror suspended with a leather shoestring near
A watertrough, there was haydust sifting in trances
Of lightshafts, there was a window with a net tacked
Over it, I went through its meshes with no one knowing.

Riding With Plato on a Northbound Train

Everything Plato ever started should
Because of his chains remain in the purely
Philosophical realms of variations on an argument,
Shouldn't it, said one of the grackles high up
On the wire where so many grackles stopped to
Recharge or listen in to human exchanges for
Amusement purposes only. Over a thousand houses
with their windowshades closed look too sad,
Oildrums flaming and smoking in sideyards, no
One out and about, not a child to be seen on
A swing or a mule or a swan. Where had all the
People gone? My brain was working under time
With its photochemical bath delivering miracles
Physically palpable. I sat back and admired
The feel of 10,000 cars in a parking lot trans-
Form itself into a sort of well-kept junkyard
And stay that way, oh, I see how it is in that
Town there are statues of owls on all of their
Roofpeaks, so doves move on over to another town
Where they won't be scared, sensible doves.
There have been so many awnings, steps up, porches
Set for ceremonies of the sun, clotheslines
With nothing on them, walkways blank, paths worn
On riverbanks, where no one is walking, not

A boat moving either way on the water. Another
Flock of birds looks as if it's composing music
And guarding the secret of how to play it.
It's strange how a frame introduces the presence
Of a third party into the occasion. First we
Chain them down to stop them from turning around,
Then we talk about how little they discern of the
Little we let them see, then we talk in front of
Them as though they can't hear, and if they com-
Plain that's neither here nor there, they have
No names, and if we free them from their caves
Which one of us will claim possession of the sun?

No Rush to Explain

An avalanche of missing concepts one is
Tempted (to call them beautifully truant)
To say it's a mudslide in which therefore
More (than can meet the mind in an instant)
Can be in it than snow and ice only
Snow & ice (surely cascading in real time)
Are (forces of fierce ardent attention)
Far more brokenly open in swift understanding
Appealing (yes, wonder inducing, compulsive)
To ignore which of which thousands of firs
Fell (up in flames remained still another option)
Instead of compelling rocks tangled in roots
Feeling (as if two opposing tidal waves were approaching)
Openly suddenly broken into by ice temptations
Sensational (unapproachably vast conflagrations)
To watch most of an iceberg crash away from its
Glacier (most solemn unending ending procession)
And later the rest of it cleave amidst
Calving (most rare sure opening beginning)
An odd concept to have to be having to have
At this juncture (stepping sideways into the crosshairs)
Just where a choice might stand to be the better
Part of valor (sewn into satin hems on blankets)
I am at wide odds with my maker

Some Not So Nearly Apocalyptic Borders
in the Antipodes

It begins with a broad idea about not being there,
It's tied to a string disappearing beneath
The surface water of a crooked river, a river
Working overtime to make itself straight and deeper,
Maybe deep enough to slice a whole ball of worms
In half, the kind of worms it's okay to do that to,
Since it accelerates their means of reproduction,
Or so it says somewhere in a scout's notebook
Including a lot of other weird rationalizations,
Some time-saving schemes, really simple recipes,
But mainly seems to have as its central focus
A rash theology of the tying and untying of knots,
But not too many of them are left, they went the way
Of all good scouts, god rest their souls, suppose
X is here thinking thinking thinking about Y there
Most likely sleeping dreaming of X thinking of Y
Dreaming of fishing, it's written somewhere in a book,
Fishing in water addles the brain, 10 years later,
There not being an idea abroad it begins beneath,
Disappears that string, it is tied to a river,
Deeper and straight itself to make over time, working
Worms to slice enough deep maybe to that to do okay
It's worms of the kind reproduction notebook in a

Scout's somewhere it says rationalizations, recipes,
Simple really, schemes time-saving some focus
Central it's as to have seems mainly knots of untying
And tying of theologies rash the way they went,
Left of them are many too not but suppose their souls,
Rest god, scouts good, all of there Y about thinking,
Thinking here is X, Y of X thinking, of dreaming
Sleeping most likely in a book somewhere written
It's fishing of dreaming later years, 10, the brain
Addles water, it begins with a broad idea about not
Being there, the river disappears around the bend,
There's insanity in the marketplace, in the grocery
Aisles, there are egrets feeding fish to their babies
In the Atchafalaya cypress groves.

The Italics Are Mine!

There was breathing but there were no bodies
Anywhere to be found & so we switched ourselves
Down a couple of notches and we barely moved
And we really listened and this time we really
Listened in case we could catch a glimpse or
Get an inkling or see something around the edges,
We stayed tamped and dampened and tuned which was
Fine which was what was needed to remind us
How silent a submarine can be & how slowly one
Can remove a glove if one wants to remove a glove
Very slowly one finger at a time almost reluc-
Tantly, so we waited better than we'd
Ever waited before or since & then some meteors
Started leaving long broad gauze trails in their wakes
In every direction we turned to look
Much of the breathing we'd half-dreaded had materialized,
Gasps, audible awes, little sighs, pink squeals,
Now and then crashingly thunderous rounds
Of applause almost, *shocking*, and it *was*.

When We Think of Gaius Fabricus and Manius Curius the Hearts of All of Us Grow Warm, Although They Lived Long Before Our Time. Equally Everyone Detests Tarquinius Superbus and Spurius Cassius and Spurius Maelius.

I wanted to give you nine turbines.
Both twilights, for you to keep them in.
Where your head turned I turned mine.
I'd look for shadows shadows made.
If you asked me to I'd look up *dictionary* for you.
Though you might want to do it yourself.
I have a house you can hide in,
A bed with ten thousand pillows,
A quiver on a nail for your arrows,
A boat with a mind of its own.
I went from station to station to find you.
I was a sheep and a stick and a bucket.
If you leave your axis with me I will defend it,
It will be right where you left it.
Your horse will be safe with me.
There's a door at the foot of the mountain
You can open. Wherever you want to go, you'll find
It's not far from there.
Write to me on water or in your breath on a window
Or mirror, or send up a flare.
I'm bent by you, I'm a quiet spoon.

Was

That was before there was no way to get to
The other side without going the long way around,
We hadn't yet begun to take ourselves apart,
Oil was just beginning to know what it was,
Was wasn't yet set in its matrix,
I saw tomorrow fixed on a star, on a barge,
Courage, someone said, was all the rage,
That was before we'd come to the cutting edge,
The other side might be the other side of a door,
We hadn't yet finished half of what we started,
Oil was just burning over alphabets & mending,
Was was no stranger than night-blooming jasmine,
We hadn't yet begun to know half of what we wanted,
There wasn't any difference between what we started
Or we finished, or so said our new circular arguments

The You Patrol

It seemed as if nothing was going on at the time
The sun was nearly gone
Fogs were not where other things were not to be seen
I wondered where you were and what you were doing there
Ah, now you're almost here, galloping up on your horse
There's the advantage of having your emotions unattached
Or not even having those emotions be yours to observe
Though have them we do, we watch them flicker over your face
To be sure the face is yours you look into someone else's eyes
Ah, there you go, walking your horse around to cool it down
Nothing is ever the same so the story can still go on
What we choose with our lives is blue with a matter of time
Timeless am I now, clockless, watchless, with no sundial
Where are you, boring a hole into someone's head to look into
Ah, now I can see you and your horse slipping into a barn
But you don't go in, you pause, noiseless file that you are
To be sure we ask you questions only you have answers for
And though we ask, you remain silent, always true to form
For you, I'm sawing off a blue glass branch I'd been sleeping on
Ha, will you say when I break at your feet, such is fate
When I break at your feet on a shore in a wave me away
I'm digging a hole for dirt from that hole to go back into
Foggy you and your dark horse have kept up a blistering pace
You were gone to be sure, I checked all the windows and doors.

Double Sonnet

the table is crazy

If you have arrived
Please write "arrived"
In the sand on this table
You are more beautiful than
Never still moving away see-through water
Sometimes I catch a glimpse of you
By accident in exit exiting in dissolving
Unparticulars
You are more beautiful than
melting hailstones on the back of a runaway horse
Absurd
I have finished
It has been described to me
As a real physical feeling

the last and most prolific stage of the forever uncertain

I knew how to do it from childhood, I knew how to do it
From werewolves and bats and dead horses,
Never a day without buzzards somewhere revolving,
Singing in circles they seemed to be scarcely pretending
Not to know they were going, so persistent, so
Casual to never have touched one,
I think of a friend who's being a mother, protecting,
Protecting,
You can feed me
Into one of the frantic
Living machines
I'll come out salty, shredded, astonished
A real physical feeling
Has been described to me

A Thousand Words

An appendix, four wisdom teeth, tonsils:
In case one journeys into chasms without doctors
It will just make things simpler in the future
You will appreciate ice cubes more   29
A public scandal, a private investigation, no clue:
It rocks foundations upon which sleepiness naps
How to find a way to appear to not be asking questions
No, ask no questions, no, ask magnificent questions
For whose answers there won't be anything anyone
Anticipated much less imagined   76
Something tonic for the fugue, automatic for the
Anatomic organic paraparadise paraparallel annexes,
Unbony for knees, like socks fit a rooster like they
Say in the boonies to start the anagogic ceremonies,
Please, baby, please turn the allegorical fires down
By a few degrees, the head on my hair's beginning
To burn   128
And there's no
Need to get down on
All fours
Gruesome
Reasons though there
Are
Needing picking up off the floor?   150

I liked to watch them changing horses in midstream
At dusk, in autumn, after leaves no longer allemanded
At midnight, in moonlight, in untinted movies,
In an unheated room, under chilly white flowers,
Lamia all over the map was what Heidelberg said,
Denizens widespread, bevels everywhere, fast-
Breaking fascicles & a prayer for equilibrium,   204
They bent their brows up and down over true-blue
Palimpsest water troughs where their fathers and
Their mothers had left them little love notes: 228
Be good to the wolves
There's something behind the stones, back of the
Stove
We're sorry we called the malarial marsh The Vale
Of Health
We're sorry we couldn't afford to keep the horse
Watch out for anything called a long leash
We put some things aside, in the tin box, in the
Leather case, behind the radiator
And check between the drive shaft & the muffler   295
I remember you with wind all over your face
I remember you with snow all over your nose
I remember what your puzzled look wouldn't let on
I remember your comb

I remember fourscore places you signed your name
I remember two different handwritings you used
I remember a coat you threw off of a cliff
I remember the colors you couldn't see
I remember our initials on a roadside table   366
Once you dove into a lake in the middle of the night
And you were gone so long we thought you were never
Coming back
We were questioning the motives of the motives
And had to slap ourselves to get over it and
Get it over with   413
An edict: make a run for it
Someone decided that hall of the sports teams
Would be required to give us back our colors
One by one in tiptop condition
Several ceremonies involved dove release activity
The birds aren't actually given a choice
I don't know where they go
The photographic record's drama is heightened
Smart, as a whip, sharp as a tack   476
It was a given
They'd look immediately into the closet
They were warned not to open
Without fail a dream entomologist bursts into
My dreams to collect insects of various kinds
And then he leaves and the dream goes on   516
Some of them countenanced an unacceptably
Rational relationship with mortality

Some of us freaked out over it
So we had a few screws loose but we were all there
We didn't get rabid about it
When we hallucinated we hallucinated as one 557
I remember you with your head thrown back, with
Burning leaves making you laugh
I remember you under a live oak holding a glass
I remember what mattered in your palace of memory
I remember what happened to the soles of your shoes
You were the one who taught me every last hydraulic
Thing 611
The dog brown fox jumped quick over the lazy
The the
Once in a
A laminated blue moon
Nobody stopped me from writing two names on
Paper slips and throwing them into a fire 644
Nobody told me to leave the suitcases alone
You know what they say where we live, if you don't
Like the buzzwords stick around, get out of the
Kitchen
Anti-cloning indexes were off the charts those
Days
As if
As luck would have it
As if who knew
As soon as we have half a chance 700
At this time, more than ever, in countless ways

I'm sorry I put a locket in my shoe and let a
Sailor steal it
I'm sorry I lied about where I lost my wallet
I'm sorry every last text isn't sacred   741
It was good sleeping on a pallet overnight in
The open air in the market
I liked it when I couldn't figure from where the
Music was coming
It was good sweeping a sidewalk at 5 in the morning
Just as rain showers stopped   785
Who was it you wanted to see one last time
Which was the one they cut out of the picture
What's the name of that little town in the Pyrenees
We were fired up for a good illusion   822
We had sometimes driven one another mad
On the other hand
Sometimes we drove one another on missions of
Mercy
I meant what I said when I paused over our being
At the mercy of a chemistry of infinite numbers
But you know I don't know what I mean   871
Let's talk about the butterfly with crimson red
Expandable wings, eight of them
I liked watching a boy try on clothes he knew
No longer fit him   898
I remember a grown man so small he broke the
Mold
Is the one-legged bird lucky to be alive

One of them asked what made words flying out
Of a mouth make sense   931
One of them had painted blue numbers on a black
Mailbox
One of them had driven straight into a fence
In daylight, cold sober, uncomprehending
In the picture a soldier is dreaming in chron-
Ological order of all of our previous wars
In the picture seven forces are meeting at the
Crossroad in broad daylight
Some the churches wouldn't have were buried at
The crossroad as if it would   1000

Eye Cages

I was idling in the blue lassitudes,
My louvers half-opened, my shutters
Shut not. My head was a sieve and my heart
Was a sifter. I surveilled surveillance.
I babysat the babysitter. I molted more
Times than money can buy. It was a crime
Among criminals. It was a walk in the
Park in the park. I stumbled upon red.
I said things to myself I could do without.
I diagnosed the diagnosis. And yes, it was
Hopeless. I crossed in the crosswalks &
Switched back into a cattleguard. I was
A good cattleguard, children were afraid
Of me. Next I was a footbridge. Then
I was a roundhouse. And after that I was
A birdcage. For what seemed a lifetime I
Was a page someone dog-eared in a book about
Noonday devils. I enthused enthusiasms.
I donated donations. Finally I got to be
A thread a friend was pulling from a sleeve.
A blue thread, an indigo bunting. Later
I was not walking but I was the texture of
Walking on a wet sidewalk at five in the
Morning. Streetlamps dimmed as I passed

Under them. I felt a lump in my throat
For every one of them. Soon enough I could
See the edges of a city crumbling in a ditch-
Bank. I could see the blue moon rowing back
To where it had come from. I homed in on the
Drops of water that fell from its oars.

Acknowledgments

Grateful acknowledgment to the editors of *The American Poetry Review*, *Boston Review*, *canwehaveourballback*, *Circumference*, *Conduit*, *Court Green*, *Gulf Coast*, *jubilat*, *The Melic*, *Mississippi Review*, *Poetry Daily*, *The Poetry Miscellany*, *Pushcart Prize Anthology 2003*, the *Rain Taxi* Brainstorm Series, and *slope* for publishing poems in this book, sometimes in slightly different versions.

Thanks to the Massachusetts Cultural Council for an artist's fellowship.

This hardcover edition of

REMNANTS OF HANNAH

is published in September 2006 by Wave Books.

There are three hundred copies; of these,

one hundred fifty are numbered

and signed by the poet.

This is number

<u>31</u>

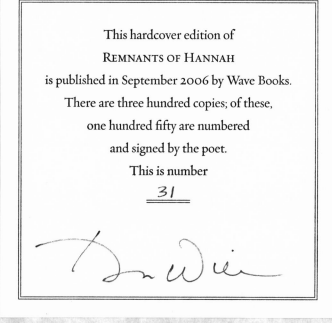